# MEDITATIONS FOR HEALING

*Activating the Power of Scriptural Meditation for Divine Healing*

Derry L. Moten

# MEDITATIONS FOR HEALING

*Activating the Power of Scriptural Meditation for Divine Healing*

*Dedication*
*I dedicate this book to my wife Tammie.  A man cannot ask for any greater support than what you have been for me. You are P31.*

*I love you.*

# CONTENTS

Introduction .................................................................. 1

God Wants You Well ...................................................... 5

Thy will be done ............................................................ 11

Meditation: the Key to Healing. ................................... 19

Scriptures for Mediation and Declaration ................. 27

Healing in the Book of Matthew ................................. 35

Healing in the Book of Mark........................................ 39

Healing in the Book of Luke ........................................ 43

Healing in the Book of John ........................................ 51

Healing in the Book of Acts......................................... 55

Conclusion..................................................................... 61

Journal ........................................................................... 63

Healing Confessions .................................................... 65

21 Day Meditations for Healing .................................. 69

# INTRODUCTION

As a person that has spent the majority of my adult life in ministry, I believe that the message of scripture is very clear.

**Hebrews 13:8**
[8] Jesus Christ is the same yesterday, today, and forever.
*NKJV*

The ministry of Jesus Christ has not changed since he ascended into the heavens as recorded in the Book of Acts chapter 1. That ministry was the same ministry that he shared with his disciples while he trained them for their eventual works of service. The ministry that Jesus had was the ministry of reconciliation.

To reconcile something means that you reestablish a close relationship, or to settle or resolve a matter. The ministry of reconciliation is God's service to mankind of reestablishing right relationship between Him and us through the sacrificial life, death, and resurrection of Jesus Christ.

Jesus has reconciled God and man and resolved a variety of issues concerning us. The first is the issue of the sin nature. Jesus has liberated us from the penalty of the nature of sin within us. We are no longer sinners, but we now walk in the Righteousness of Christ. The second is the power of sin to rule over our lives. We were once slaves of sin, but now we have the power to choose to live for God in Holiness.

There are many other areas, of reconciliation and redemption; the one we will focus on in this text is Healing. The Gospels of Matthew, Mark, Luke, and John illustrate the Good News of Jesus Christ. One of the most overwhelming characteristics of Jesus' ministry is the ministry of healing.

As you read on I ask that you put aside your preconceived notions and let the Word of God speak to you. Meditate on what the Word says and let God have His perfect work in you.

After taking the step of faith to put this text together, I was attacked by generational disease; I did not accept or receive it. I sought out God's answers and the Word of God is clear:

> **1 Peter 2:21-24**
> [21] For to this you were called, because Christ also suffered for us, leaving us an example, that you should follow His steps:
>
> [22] "Who committed no sin,
> Nor was deceit found in His mouth";
>
> [23] who, when He was reviled, did not revile in return; when He suffered, He did not threaten, but committed Himself to Him who judges righteously; [24] who Himself bore our sins in His own body on the tree, that we, having died to sins, might live for righteousness-- ___by whose stripes you were healed.___ NKJV

Just as sure as I have been made righteous, I am healed. If you believe in Jesus as your Lord and Savior, you are healed. It is not only God's will, it is God's provision for us in Jesus Christ.

Understanding that healing has been provided for you is only the first step. Next you will have to receive the spiritual revelation of this truth through daily meditation and confession, and with courage and diligence apply the truth to your life and personal situation.

> ***Proverbs 18:21***
> Death and life are in the power of the tongue,
> And those who love it will eat its fruit.

When this happens, you will see the manifestation of your healing, and God will make you a witness of Jesus' ministry of healing. Your testimony will impart this truth and God's love to others who are awaiting your testimony to help them. The words from your mouth will set others free.

Receive your healing, walk in your healing, declare your healing because you are healed.

> *For to this you were called, because Christ also suffered for us, leaving us an example, that you should follow His steps: 22 Who committed no sin, Nor was deceit found in His mouth"; 23 who, when He was reviled, did not revile in return; when He suffered, He did not threaten, but committed Himself to Him who judges righteously; 24 who Himself bore our sins in His own body on the tree, that we, having died to sins, might live for righteousness—by whose stripes you were healed.*

# GOD WANTS YOU WELL

*Chapter 1*

> *Jeremiah 29:11*
> *For I know the thoughts that I think toward you, says the Lord, thoughts of peace and not of evil, to give you a future and a hope. NKJV*

God wants to heal us and keep us well.

Many times we (the church) do not realize how far the natural mind of man has drifted or been driven away from the thoughts and mind of the Almighty God.

> **Isaiah 55:8**
> "For My thoughts are not your thoughts,
> Nor are your ways My ways," Says the Lord.

We clearly see it in the lives and actions of people that grossly violate the natural laws of men, committing crimes and atrocities against others and themselves in the earth. But we do not so clearly identify it in our own lives when we live beneath the intended life that God desires for us in Christ Jesus.

Both the natural and ungodly spiritual influences of the world draw us away from the plans and purposes of God. Many of these influences boldly and subtly create images in our minds that normalize the power of sin and death with us. This occurs in our acceptance of the authority of the sin nature, sickness and disease, poverty and lack, emotional and mental weakness, division and strife, and each of their corresponding offshoots and offspring. Being born as natural men and women in the earth we are subject to these laws. They are the governing laws of mankind, under the curse that abides in the earth that stems back to the fall of Adam and Eve. The natural man lives under the authority of these things and is a slave to them.

But thanks be to God for what the Scriptures say in Romans 8:2, "For the law of the Spirit of Life in Christ Jesus, has made me free from the law of sin and death." There is a Law of the Spirit of Life in Christ Jesus, and that law operates on a series of basic principles that every believer must understand and learn how to operate in. The Law of the Spirit of Life in Christ Jesus is the law of total redemption. It is the law of total prosperity. It is the law that sets us free from the laws of sin and death. It is God's revealed will for His Children that have been bought with a price, the blood and body of Jesus Christ.

> ### John 3:16 - 17
> [16] God so loved the world that He gave his only begotten son, that whosoever should believe on Him, **should not perish but have everlasting life.** [17] For God did not send His son into the world to condemn the world, but that the world through Him might be saved. *NKJV*

We are told that as we meditate on "this book of the Law", and as "we observe to do all that is written therein", we shall make our way prosperous and we shall have good success. This quote from Joshua Chapter one verse eight gives us God's method for moving from the common to the blessed.  The book of Romans Chapter 12 verse 2 says that we should not be conformed to this world, but be transformed by the renewing of the mind so that we can prove the good, perfect and acceptable will of God.

### Joshua 1:8
[8] This book of the law shall not depart from your mouth, but you shall meditate on it day and night, that you may observe and do all that is written in it.  For then you shall make your way prosperous, and then you shall deal wisely and have good success. *Amplified*

### Romans 12:2
[2] Do not be conformed to this world (this age), [fashioned after and adapted to its external superficial customs], but be transformed (changed) by the [entire] renewal of your mind [by its new ideas and new attitude], so that you might prove [for yourselves] what is the good and acceptable and perfect will of God, even the thing which is good and acceptable and perfect [in His sight for you]. *Amplified*

The true Christ redeemed life of man, as intended by God, is revealed in the scriptures.  As we embrace, meditate, and act on the revelation of God's desire and plan for us, we are transformed from "mere men", to vibrant sons and daughters of God.  We take our position as eternal spiritual beings that flow in the anointing of God through the empowering of His Holy Spirit in these mortal bodies. We become living witnesses of the Life of God in the earth.

### Hebrews 4:14-16
[14] Seeing then that we have a great High Priest who has passed through the heavens, Jesus the Son of God, ***let us hold fast our***

*__confession__*. [15] For we do not have a High Priest who cannot sympathize with our weaknesses, but was in all points tempted as we are, yet without sin. [16] *__Let us therefore come boldly to the throne of grace, that we may obtain mercy and find grace to help in time of need.__* NKJV

### 2 Corinthians 12:9

[9] And He said to me, "My grace is sufficient for you, for My strength is made perfect in weakness." Therefore most gladly I will rather boast in my infirmities, that the power of Christ may rest upon me. *NKJV*

This statement by the Apostle Paul does not mean that he went around bragging that he was weak. But as Hebrews 4:15 says, we do not have a High Priest that cannot sympathize with us in our weaknesses. This sinless High Priest, not only can sympathize but by the grace of God, He leads us to the throne of the Most High, where we can come boldly with no sense of condemnation or inferiority. By coming before the throne of grace, we take the opportunity to present ourselves to God and allow Him to be strong in us.

At the throne of grace, we find real help to answer the real challenges we face in this life. This help does not come in the form of handouts or sympathetic tokens to get over for just another day, but solutions to the very nature of our problems, and the eternal cure to the manifestation of the laws of sin and death. If we dare to take our place at the throne of God and receive His instruction and direction, we will usher in the power of God to impact our lives and our world.

Many of us approach the throne of grace in fear, rather than in faith. This is especially true in situations where we have received a report of terminal illness. Approaching God in fear robs us of the blessing of grace because God responds to our faith.

### Hebrews 11:6

But without faith it is impossible to please Him (God), for he who comes to God must believe that He is and that He is a rewarder of those that diligently seek Him.

The fear of death becomes a cloud to our faith and blocks our ability to receive the promise of God. Fear makes us focus on death and dying rather than focusing on our purpose and living the life that we have in Christ right now.

Every day of the Christian life should be lived purposefully, not fearful of death. Having said that, let us all face a universal reality. No one escapes the shadow of death. As Hebrews 9:27 says

### Hebrews 9:27

[27] And as it is appointed unto men once to die, but after this the judgment:

One day every person must physically die, but until that time comes, we are to walk in health and overcome all manner of sickness and disease through divine healing. This text is designed to increase your faith in the area of healing so that you can receive from God and daily be about fulfilling your God-given purpose.

# THY WILL BE DONE

*Chapter 2*

> *1 John 5:14-15*
> *Now this is the confidence that we have in Him, that if we*
> *ask anything according to His will, He hears us. ¹⁵ And if we*
> *know that He hears us, whatever we ask, we know that we*
> *have the petitions that we have asked of Him.*

What is your opinion regarding healing? Have you been persuaded that healing is a byproduct of salvation? Have you ever considered that God would perhaps want you well for the purpose of fulfilling His will for you in the earth? Have you ever heard someone say about healing, "well whatever the will of the Lord is..."?

Large populations of Christians in the world resist the teaching of divine health and healing. The leaders of these arguments are enraged when we walk into hospitals and tell people that God wants them well. They are insulted that our children who have grown up with this belief system are bold to declare this as truth and are willing to pray for the sick. They are disturbed by our boldness to restore hope to the sick and suffering, by speaking life to their situations and boldly cursing sickness and disease that attempts to eat away at their bodies and releasing faith to raise them from their beds of sickness.

The arguments against faith in this area of God's ability are not usually derived from scripture, but originate from the humanistic culture and mindsets that surround us. They originate from men's experiences or lack thereof. The tiers of these arguments being the following:

1. Believers cannot force God to move in the area of healing.
2. If God wants people healed, then He would just heal them.
3. Why build up peoples hope when we have no way of knowing if God will heal them?

The real question that we should be asking is "who and what is God?" Understanding who and what God is, will then allow us to more freely receive the true will of God for our lives.

One of the most foundational questions that any believer can ask is, "who is God?" The answer to this question can become a long discourse of theological or metaphysical theories or it can be a simple declaration of faith. Either way, the answer to this question will either aid or hinder your understanding of God's will and His ability to fulfill the promises of scripture. Your response to the Word of God will be affected by your personal heart answer to this foundational question.

### Genesis 1:1
"In the beginning God created the heavens and the earth."
NKJV

First of all, let's accept the fact that Genesis reveals that at the beginning of all creation, God existed beyond all the current limitations of our lives. He is there before time, before light, before gravity, and before illness sickness and disease. God is self-existent in our dimension because He is the creator of the very fabric of our lives. We have imposed the limitations of our humanity on God, based on our experience and human logic, but God is not a man.

### Numbers 23:19

"God is not a man, that He should lie, nor a son of man, that He should repent. Has He said, and will He not do? Or has He spoken, and will He not make it good?"   *NKJV*

God is the self-existent creator that dwells beyond the realm of human existence.  That makes God spirit.

### John 4:24

"God is Spirit, and those who worship Him must worship in spirit and truth."  *NKJV*

In the book of Numbers, the Children of Israel faced our same challenge.  They were forced to change their lenses concerning the issue of God's identity and His ability to fulfill His Word which reveals His will.  Because God is spirit, to receive His Word we must do so, in spirit and truth.

In Exodus chapter 15, God is speaking to the Children of Israel and Moses, declaring to them that He is their healer.

### Exodus 15:26

"If you diligently heed the voice of the Lord your God and do what is right in His sight, give ear to His commandments and keep all of His statutes, I will put none of the diseases on you which I have brought on the Egyptians, for I am the Lord who heals you."

In this passage, God reveals His own character as a healer.

Most believers are familiar with Jesus' model prayer that he provided to the disciples. This prayer is found in Matthew 6:9-13.

> ### *Matthew 6: 9-13*
> [9]"Our Father in Heaven,
> Hallowed be Your name.
> [10] Your kingdom come
> Your will be done,
> On earth as it is in heaven.
> [11] Give us this day our daily bread.
> [12] And forgive us our debts,
> As we forgive our debtors.
> [13] And do not lead us into temptation,
> But deliver us from the evil one.
> For yours is the kingdom and the power, and the glory forever.
> Amen." *NKJV*

Jesus provides the disciples with this powerful key to addressing the Father in prayer. Not praying with natural vain repetitions but going to the heart of God and communicating with Him by faith, in the areas that matter the most. Worship, submission, provision, avoiding temptation, deliverance, and forgiveness are all addressed in this prayer. In praying all these things we all know that there is no deliverance without the one that is bound taking a stand. There is no provision for the one that will not stand in faith and engage in the appropriate activities that will bring about provision. There is no forgiveness for those that will not walk in forgiveness, and the will of God cannot and will not be manifested unless someone prays and seeks the Godly answer.

> ### Matthew 6: 10
> [10] "Your kingdom come,
> Your will be done,
> On earth as it is in heaven."

No one will dispute that the will of God is done in heaven. The will of God being done on the Earth is a different issue. If Jesus told the disciples that they would have to pray that the will of God be done in the earth, does that not suggest that the will of God being done in the Earth is not automatic. There is resistance in the Earth to the will of God being done. In case we have not considered this, please remember that the world lies under the authority and control of the evil one (devil). You may have to fight to get it, but healing is the will of God. Anything that God desires to give you will be met with resistance from the adversary, but our fight with him is not with flesh and blood, but the good fight of faith in the spirit.

For the will of God to be done on the Earth there must be an agent in the Earth to bring about change. God must use an agent that has received the legal right to exercise authority in the Earth. Without such an agent there can be no operation of God's will on the Earth. God has chosen us to be those agents of His power and glory in the Earth. Through the blood of Jesus, we have been given the legal right to exercise dominion over sickness and disease in the earth.

> ### 1 Peter 2:24-25
> [24] who Himself bore our sins in His own body on the tree, that we, having died to sins, might live for righteousness--_by whose stripes you were healed_. [25] For you were like sheep going

astray, but have now returned to the Shepherd and Overseer of your souls.  *NKJV*

In this passage, Peter mentions the forgiveness of our sins and identifies that by His stripes you were healed.  Who is he speaking to?  To you the reader!

**1 Peter 2:24b**
[24] .....--by whose stripes you were healed..   *NKJV*

Your healing is provided for in the same sacrifice that your salvation was acquired through.  "You were healed", this is past tense and speaks to a work completed already.  Jesus has already made the provision for you.  Please do not make the mistake of believing that just because something is easy it is the will of God, or because something is challenging or difficult, that God is not in it.

The fight you are engaged in is the renewing of your mind so that the will of God may be manifested in you.  Human effort is not the fruit that can change your life.  Renewing our minds and receiving the Word of God will release us into the supernatural realm of the spirit, where God has no limits and we can freely drink from the wells of salvation and healing.

My personal experience with this reality came while writing the foundations of this book. I received the revelation that God was my healer through my redemption in Christ and began to write that reality for a message that I was planning.  The revelation began to take shape and right in the middle of my writing, I was tested.

I found myself laying in a hospital bed with a nurse telling me that I should have been in a coma. But I was not in a coma, I was alert and aware. The nurse shared with me that I should have arrived at the hospital in an ambulance, but I walked into the hospital by my own power, yet, not my power but Christ in me. The Word in my heart and mind was empowering me to defy the dominion of the disease. A disease was attacking my body, but my Spirit was sustaining me. The same spirit that raised Christ from the dead, was empowering me to be an overcomer in the moment. The Word that I meditated on when I was well, was sustaining me through the attack.

In this season of crisis, the Word of God kept coming up in my Spirit. "By His stripes we are healed". As the Word kept coming up, I continued to meditate on the reality of the Word, and eventually the Holy Spirit spoke to me with instructions.

It was at this point that I came to understand that I cannot and will not leave this earth until my purpose is fulfilled. That understanding helped me overcome the spirit of fear and obey the Holy Spirit's directions. The Holy Spirit educated me on my adversary and gave me a kingdom plan of action to overcome him. I acted on the revelation and walked out of the issue.

Overcoming fear is a major issue for all that are challenged by sickness. Fear is a tormentor that is never satisfied. The presence of fear absorbs a person's energy that should be used in the healing process and diverts it into unproductive areas. When we should be in a state of gratitude for all the great things around us, instead fear has us looking to the future and envisioning the worst possible scenarios. When we should be rejoicing about the presence of God with us, fear will make a person wonder why God would abandon them.

The truth is that fear is a state of mind, that is only overcome by the renewing of our minds to receive God's provision for every challenge we face. The greatest area of renewal being our understanding of the power of our redemption.

### Hebrews 2:14-15

14 Forasmuch then as the children are partakers of flesh and blood, he also himself likewise took part of the same; that through death he might destroy him that had the power of death, that is, the devil;

15 And deliver them who through fear of death were all their lifetime subject to bondage.

If you can receive the truth of the flesh and blood of Jesus and what it means to our redemption, you can be set free from the bondage of fear, and your healing can flow.

As you meditate on these scriptures please receive them as the eternal Word of God, full of power and full of God's ability. Receive the Word of the Lord and walk in the blessing of our God. Receive the revelation that it is God's will to heal mankind of every sickness and disease. Receive the revelation that Jesus' blood was shed, and he died to bring us total redemption, which includes healing.

Because of Him (Jesus), we are healed.

# MEDITATION: THE KEY TO HEALING.

## Chapter 3

> *Joshua 1:8*
> *This book of the Law shall not depart from your mouth, but you shall meditate in it day and night, that you may observe to do all that is written in it. For then your make your way prosperous, and then you will have good success.*

Healing requires faith followed with tangible action (works). Believe you receive when you pray. But what do you do if you don't yet believe? You build your faith through meditation on the Word.

### Romans 10:17
[17] So then faith comes by hearing, and hearing by the word of God. *NKJV*

### Joshua 1:8
[8] This book of the law shall not depart from your mouth, but you shall meditate on it day and night, that you may observe and do all that is written in it. For then you shall make your way prosperous, and then you shall deal wisely and have good success. *Amplified*

Are you aware of your dominate thoughts? Meditation means to engage in though, contemplation, or reflection.  So there is focused meditation, your conscious thoughts, and your unconscious thoughts. This book offers you an opportunity to focus your meditation on the Word, but then there are your thoughts that you must also take dominion over.

As you begin following the instructions you will receive on focused meditation, you will then need to allow that focused meditation to begin impacting your conscious thoughts.  It will then begin to connect with your spirit and dominate your unconscious thoughts so that even when you are not conscious of meditating on healing, your spirit will confess your healing in your inner most being. Your confessions of the Word, will begin transforming your mind, and align you with the will of God.

## Forgiveness

The will of God is always opposed by the enemy of our souls.  One of the biggest hinderances the enemy uses to dominate our thought life and hinder personal healing, is offense. When we are offended or hurt, the thoughts of the problem tend to dominate our thinking and become a constant meditation. We tell the story over and over in our heads, and then we tell others how we were offended or victimized. Every confession of the story weakens us and fixates us on how we are victims of offense, rather than victors in Christ.

When others offend us, we must be quick to forgive and release them, otherwise the offended person is forced to bear the weight and internal stress of the offense, and many times the perpetrator walks away ignorant of the impact. Many of us who have been offended in the past find that the wound causes our unconscious mind to hold on waiting for resolution. If none comes from the offender, then our hurt or anger kick in and begin formulating ways to resolve the issue. Usually these ways involve revenge or retribution. In either case, the power within which should be used to meditate on our healing is being zapped by this negative energy that is moving us in the wrong direction.

The sacrifice of Jesus brings us complete forgiveness, so that we can be forgiving of others. Unforgiveness unchecked, eventually becomes bitterness, and it defiles and derails many people.

### Hebrews 12:14-15
14 Follow peace with all men, and holiness, without which no man shall see the Lord:
15 Looking diligently lest any man fail of the grace of God; lest any root of bitterness springing up trouble you, and thereby many be defiled;

As you are meditating on the Word, release anyone who has offended or hurt you. Receive God's forgiveness and use your forgiveness to forgive others. Are you waiting for an apology? Forgive before they ask, because the responsibility of forgiveness is on the person that has been offended. Don't wait for them to ask for forgiveness, use the example of Jesus hanging on the cross.

### Luke 23:34
Then said Jesus, Father, forgive them; for they know not what they do. And they parted his raiment, and cast lots.

While the soldiers were hanging Him on the cross, mocking Him, and dividing His clothes, Jesus was forgiving them. He was releasing them as He was preparing to die at their hands. But He was able to forgive, because He was committing Himself to the Father, who He knew was a healer and able to raise Him from the death He was about to suffer. Look to Jesus, beyond the offense that you have suffered, and consider the joy and impact of your healing, and you will find that releasing others is not as hard as you think. He is our example.

> ### *Hebrews 12:2-4*
> [2] Looking unto Jesus the author and finisher of our faith; who for the joy that was set before him endured the cross, despising the shame, and is set down at the right hand of the throne of God.
> [3] For consider him that endured such contradiction of sinners against himself, lest ye be wearied and faint in your minds.
> [4] Ye have not yet resisted unto blood, striving against sin.

Forgive and prepare to walk in your healing. Don't let a root of bitterness keep you from God's promise of healing to you. Keep your meditation on the Word, not on offenses.

## Start Your Meditation

As you prepare to meditate on the Word of God please remember the following:

- Take your time and really meditate about what you are reading. Although we live a life of faith, the scriptures lead us to a logical conclusion concerning God's will towards healing.

- Pray for God to enlighten your mind to the truth concerning His will in the area of Healing. If it is true, then let God persuade you through His Word. What people say apart from the scriptures is only conceptual and personal opinion. Trust in God and His Word.

- Act on God's instructions immediately. As God communicates back to you be prepared to respond immediately.

- As Joshua 1:8 says, do not let the word depart from your mouth. Speak God's Word concerning healing. Boldly declare it to your body. Declare it to your mind. Confess the Word to God, as it says in Hebrews 4:14 "...let us hold fast our confession".

- As you confess the Word, say out loud what the Word is saying to you. Faith comes by hearing, and as you hear yourself your faith will increase.

- According to II Corinthians 10:4-5, reject any thoughts or confessions that go against what God reveals to you from His Word, especially any thoughts of unforgiveness.

### II Corinthians 10:4-5

For the weapons of our warfare are not carnal but mighty in God for pulling down strongholds, casting down arguments and every high thing that exalts itself against the knowledge of God, bringing every thought into captivity to the obedience of Christ. *NKJV*

- Don't stop! Once you begin making your confession of faith, continue to confess and thank God for the work being done. Thank God for your healing even as you take prescribed medication.

- When you believe God for your healing, begin doing what well people do. Begin eating correctly, begin exercising, begin instituting a sabbath (time of rest) in your life. Most importantly, begin living your God-given life and fulfill your Kingdom purpose.

It is important to understand that God has given each person a measure of faith. When Jesus' disciples struggled with tasks, His question to them was, "where is your faith?" The observation here being, He knew that they had faith, but what were they believing?

Usually our faith follows our meditation. The things that we meditate on and confess are the things that dominate our thinking and as a result, find avenues for manifestation.

So, what if we could focus our thoughts/meditations and bring them into alignment with the will of God? We would be bringing the power of human abilities and aligning them with the eternal omnipotent power of God. This is the power of meditations for healing. Bringing our soul into alignment with the Spirit of God so that we overcome every sickness and disease.

### Psalm 103:1-5
Bless the LORD, O my soul;
And all that is within me, *bless* His holy name!
² Bless the LORD, O my soul, And forget not all His benefits:
³ Who forgives all your iniquities, Who heals all your diseases,

⁴Who redeems your life from destruction,
Who crowns you with lovingkindness and tender mercies,
⁵Who satisfies your mouth with good *things,*
*So that* your youth is renewed like the eagle's.

To "bless the Lord" is to speak well of Him, or to speak aloud that which we know about Him. This passage tells us not to forget (mindset) all of His benefits. Forgiveness, healing, redemption, lovingkindness and tender mercies, satisfaction, and renewing of our youth. These things are right at the tip of our tongue. Just waiting for us to the bless the Lord.

Get God's Word in your heart, so that it becomes the confession of your mouth.

# SCRIPTURES FOR MEDIATION AND DECLARATION

## *Chapter 4*

> *Matthew 8:8*
> *The centurion answered and said, Lord, I am not worthy that You should come under my roof. But only speak a word, and my servant will be healed.*

If you have been following the reality of what we are saying here then you know by now that at some point the only way to benefit from this revelation is to apply it to your life. Over the next several chapters, you will find scriptures and passages that validate God's will concerning healing. Your objective is to receive this revelation and begin activating it through meditation and declaration. Your faith will receive the truth and release God's healing anointing all over you. With your mouth you will bring the manifestation of the growing faith in your heart.

At the end of this book we have included a 21-day journal to help you activate your meditation and declaration journey.

If you have received a bad report from your doctor, then use your meditations as an addition to the medical prescriptions that the doctor prescribes. Your body is designed to heal itself, and your meditations free your body from stresses and allow God's perfect design to work. Ask any doctor and they will tell you that the medications are dependent on your body agreeing and responding to treatment. Your meditation on God's Word will engage your spirit and soul in bringing your body health.

### 3 John 1-2
² Beloved, I pray that you may prosper in all things and be in health, just as your soul prospers. *NKJV*

### Ps 107:20
²⁰ He sent His word and <u>healed them,</u>
And delivered them from their destructions. *NKJV*

### Ps 103:2-5
² Bless the LORD, O my soul, And forget not all His benefits:
³ Who forgives all your iniquities, Who <u>heals all your diseases,</u>
⁴ Who redeems your life from destruction, Who crowns you with loving-kindness and tender mercies,
⁵ Who satisfies your mouth with good things, So that your youth is renewed like the eagle's. *NKJV*

### Ex 15:26
²⁶ and said, "If you diligently heed the voice of the LORD your God and do what is right in His sight, give ear to His commandments and keep all His statutes, I will put none of the diseases on you which I have brought on the Egyptians. For I am the LORD who heals you." (Jehovah Rapha) *NKJV*

### Ex 23:24-26
²⁴ You shall not bow down to their gods, nor serve them, nor do according to their works; but you shall utterly overthrow

them and completely break down their sacred pillars. 25 So you shall serve the LORD your God, and He will bless your bread and your water. And I will take sickness away from the midst_of you._ <sup>26</sup> No one shall suffer miscarriage or be barren in your land; I will fulfill the number of your days. *NKJV*

### Phil 1:6

<sup>6</sup> being confident of this very thing, that He who has begun a good work in you will complete it until the day of Jesus Christ; *NKJV*

### Ps 91:14-16

<sup>14</sup> "Because he has set his love upon Me, therefore I will deliver him;
I will set him on high, because he has known My name.
<sup>15</sup> He shall call upon Me, and I will answer him;
I will be with him in trouble; I will deliver him and honor him.
<sup>16</sup> With long life I will satisfy him, And show him My salvation." *NKJV*

### Isa 53:4-5

<sup>4</sup> Surely He has borne our griefs (sickness)
And carried our sorrows (afflictions);
Yet we esteemed Him stricken,
Smitten by God, and afflicted.
<sup>5</sup> But He was wounded for our transgressions,
He was bruised for our iniquities;
The chastisement for our peace was upon Him,
And by His stripes we are healed. *NKJV*

### Isa 54:17

[17] _No weapon formed against you shall prosper_, And every tongue which rises against you in judgment You shall condemn. This is the heritage of the servants of the LORD, And their righteousness is from Me," Says the LORD.  *NKJV*

### Mal 3:11

[11] "And _I will rebuke the devourer for your sakes_, So that he will not destroy the fruit of your ground, Nor shall the vine fail to bear fruit for you in the field," Says the LORD of hosts;  *NKJV*

### John 10:9-11

[9] I am the door. If anyone enters by Me, he will be saved, and will go in and out and find pasture. 10 The thief does not come except to steal, and to kill, and to destroy. I have come that they may have life, and that they may have it more abundantly. *NKJV*

### Matt 12:28-30

[29] Or how can one enter a strong man's house and plunder his goods, unless he first binds the strong man? And then he will plunder his house.  *NKJV*

### Matt 15:22-28

[22] And behold, a woman of Canaan came from that region and cried out to Him, saying, "Have mercy on me, O Lord, Son of David! My daughter is severely demon-possessed." [23] But He answered her not a word. And His disciples came and urged Him, saying, "Send her away, for she cries out after us." [24] But He answered and said, "I was not sent except to the lost sheep of the house of Israel." [25] Then she came and worshiped

Him, saying, "Lord, help me!" ²⁶ But He answered and said, "It is not good to take the children's bread and throw it to the little dogs." ²⁷ And she said, "Yes, Lord, yet even the little dogs eat the crumbs which fall from their masters' table." ²⁸ Then Jesus answered and said to her, _"O woman, great is your faith! Let it be to you as you desire." And her daughter was healed from that very hour_. *NKJV*

### Rev 1:5-7

⁵ and from Jesus Christ, the faithful witness, the firstborn from the dead, and the ruler over the kings of the earth. To Him who loved us and washed us from our sins in His own blood, ⁶ _and has made us kings and priests to His God and Father_, to Him be glory and dominion forever and ever. Amen. *NKJV*

### Job 22:23-30

²³ _If you return to the Almighty, you will be built up;_ You will remove iniquity far from your tents. ²⁴ Then you will lay your gold in the dust, And the gold of Ophir among the stones of the brooks. ²⁵ Yes, the Almighty will be your gold And your precious silver; ²⁶ For then you will have your delight in the Almighty, And lift up your face to God. ²⁷ _You will make your prayer to Him, He will hear you_, And you will pay your vows. ²⁸ _You will also declare a thing, And it will be established for you_; So light will shine on your ways.

²⁹ When they cast you down, and you say, 'Exaltation will come!' Then He will save the humble person. ³⁰ He will even deliver one who is not innocent; Yes, he will be delivered by the purity of your hands." *NKJV*

*Matt 21:21-22*

²¹ So Jesus answered and said to them, "Assuredly, I say to you, <u>if you have faith and do not doubt</u>, you will not only do what was done to the fig tree, but also <u>if you say to this mountain</u>, 'Be removed and be cast into the sea,' <u>it will be done</u>. *NKJV*

*Matt 21:18-22*

¹⁸ Now in the morning, as He returned to the city, He was hungry. ¹⁹ And seeing a fig tree by the road, He came to it and found nothing on it but leaves, and said to it, "Let no fruit grow on you ever again." And immediately the fig tree withered away.

²⁰ And when the disciples saw it, they marveled, saying, "How did the fig tree wither away so soon?" ²¹ So Jesus answered and said to them, "Assuredly, I say to you, if you have faith and do not doubt, you will not only do what was done to the fig tree, but also if you say to this mountain, 'Be removed and be cast into the sea,' it will be done. ²² And *<u>whatever things you ask in prayer, believing, you will receive.</u>*" *NKJV*

*Nah 1:9*

⁹ What do you conspire against the LORD? He will make an utter end of it. *<u>Affliction will not rise up a second time.</u>* *NKJV*

*Matt 16:19-20*

¹⁹ And I will give you the keys of the kingdom of heaven, and whatever you bind on earth will be bound in heaven, and whatever you loose on earth will be loosed in heaven." *NKJV*

*Eph 6:12-13*

¹² For we do not wrestle against flesh and blood, but against principalities, against powers, against the rulers of the darkness of this age, against spiritual hosts of wickedness in the heavenly places. ¹³ Therefore take up the whole armor of God, that you may be able to withstand in the evil day, and having done all, to stand. *NKJV*

*2 Cor 10:4-6*

⁴ For the weapons of our warfare are not carnal but mighty in God for pulling down strongholds, ⁵ casting down arguments and every high thing that exalts itself against the knowledge of God, bringing every thought into captivity to the obedience of Christ, *NKJV*

*Isa 58:6*

⁶ "Is this not the fast that I have chosen: To loose the bonds of wickedness, To undo the heavy burdens, To let the oppressed go free, And that you break every yoke? *NKJV*

*1 Tim 6:15-16*

¹⁵ which He will manifest in His own time, He who is the blessed and only Potentate, the King of kings and Lord of lords, ¹⁶ who alone has immortality, dwelling in unapproachable light, whom no man has seen or can see, to whom be honor and everlasting power. Amen. *NKJV*

*James 5:16-18*

¹⁶ Confess your trespasses to one another, and pray for one another, that you may be healed. The effective, fervent prayer of a righteous man avails much. ¹⁷ Elijah was a man with a nature like ours, and he prayed earnestly that it would not

rain; and it did not rain on the land for three years and six months. ¹⁸ And he prayed again, and the heaven gave rain, and the earth produced its fruit.  *NKJV*


### Isa 55:11
¹¹ So shall My word be that goes forth from My mouth; It shall not return to Me void,
But it shall accomplish what I please, And it shall prosper in the thing for which I sent it.  *NKJV*


### Isa 53:5
⁵ But He was wounded for our transgressions, He was bruised for our iniquities;  The chastisement for our peace was upon Him,  And *by His stripes we are healed*.   *NKJV*


### 1 Peter 2:24-25
²⁴ who Himself bore our sins in His own body on the tree, that we, having died to sins, might live for righteousness--*by whose stripes you were healed*. ²⁵ For you were like sheep going astray, but have now returned to the Shepherd and Overseer of your souls.   *NKJV*

# HEALING IN THE BOOK
# OF MATTHEW

*Chapter 5*

> *Matthew 8:13*
> *Then Jesus said to the centurion, "Go your way; and as you have believed, so let it be done for you." And his servant was healed that same hour. NKJV*

Matthew is the first book of the New Testament. The author (Matthew) was a tax collector and a person that was disliked by the general population of Israel, but like the rest of us, no matter what others believe about us, God loves us and receives us, if we receive Him.

The book gives us a first look at Jesus of Nazareth, the Son of Man, who accepts the stranger and heals those in need without regard to their background or faults.

> **Matt 4: 24**
> ²⁴ Then His fame went throughout all Syria; and they brought to Him all sick people who were afflicted with various diseases and torments, and those who were demon-

possessed, epileptics, and paralytics; and He healed them. *NKJV*

### Matt 8:5-13

⁵ Now when Jesus had entered Capernaum, a centurion came to Him, pleading with Him, ⁶ saying, "Lord, my servant is lying at home paralyzed, dreadfully tormented." ⁷ And Jesus said to him, "I will come and heal him." ⁸ The centurion answered and said, "Lord, I am not worthy that You should come under my roof. But only speak a word, and my servant will be healed. ⁹ For I also am a man under authority, having soldiers under me. And I say to this one, 'Go,' and he goes; and to another, 'Come,' and he comes; and to my servant, 'Do this,' and he does it." ¹⁰ When Jesus heard it, He marveled, and said to those who followed, "Assuredly, I say to you, I have not found such great faith, not even in Israel! ¹¹ And I say to you that many will come from east and west, and sit down with Abraham, Isaac, and Jacob in the kingdom of heaven. ¹² But the sons of the kingdom will be cast out into outer darkness. There will be weeping and gnashing of teeth." ¹³ Then Jesus said to the centurion, **"Go your way; and as you have believed, so let it be done for you."** And his servant was healed that same hour. *NKJV*

### Matt 8:16-17

¹⁶ When evening had come, they brought to Him many who were demon-possessed. And He cast out the spirits with a word, and healed all who were sick, ¹⁷ that it might be fulfilled which was spoken by Isaiah the prophet, saying:

"He Himself took our infirmities, And bore our sicknesses." *NKJV*

### Matt 10:1

¹ And when He had called His twelve disciples to Him, He gave them power over unclean spirits, to cast them out, and to heal all kinds of sickness and all kinds of disease.   *NKJV*

### Matt 10:5-8

⁵ These twelve Jesus sent out and commanded them, saying: "Do not go into the way of the Gentiles, and do not enter a city of the Samaritans. ⁶ But go rather to the lost sheep of the house of Israel. ⁷ And as you go, preach, saying, 'The kingdom of heaven is at hand.' ⁸ Heal the sick, cleanse the lepers, raise the dead, cast out demons. Freely you have received, freely give.   *NKJV*

### Matt 12:15

¹⁵ But when Jesus knew it, He withdrew from there. And great multitudes followed Him, and He healed them all.   *NKJV*

### Matt 12:22

²² Then one was brought to Him who was demon-possessed, blind and mute; and He healed him, so that the blind and mute man both spoke and saw.   *NKJV*

### Matt 14:14

¹⁴ And when Jesus went out He saw a great multitude; and He was moved with compassion for them, and healed their sick. *NKJV*

*Matt 15:22-28*

²² And behold, a woman of Canaan came from that region and cried out to Him, saying, "Have mercy on me, O Lord, Son of David! My daughter is severely demon-possessed." ²³ But He answered her not a word. And His disciples came and urged Him, saying, "Send her away, for she cries out after us." ²⁴ But He answered and said, "I was not sent except to the lost sheep of the house of Israel." ²⁵ Then she came and worshiped Him, saying, "Lord, help me!" ²⁶ But He answered and said, "It is not good to take the children's bread and throw it to the little dogs." ²⁷ And she said, "Yes, Lord, yet even the little dogs eat the crumbs which fall from their masters' table." ²⁸ Then Jesus answered and said to her, "O woman, great is your faith! Let it be to you as you desire." And her daughter was healed from that very hour. *NKJV*

*Matt 15:30*

³⁰ Then great multitudes came to Him, having with them the lame, blind, mute, maimed, and many others; and they laid them down at Jesus' feet, and He healed them. *NKJV*

*Matt 19:2*

² And great multitudes followed Him, and He healed them there. *NKJV*

*Matt 21:14*

¹⁴ Then the blind and the lame came to Him in the temple, and He healed them. *NKJV*

# HEALING IN THE BOOK OF MARK

*Chapter 6*

> *Mark 5: 34*
> *And He said to her, "Daughter, your faith has made you well. Go in peace, and be healed of your affliction." NKJV*

The book of Mark is primarily written to an audience of people outside of Judaism (gentiles like most of us). His observations of Jesus reveal the character of a servant of humanity. Not religious in approach but concerned about the lives of people. The book shows Jesus in action and not theory, therefore we see examples of His healing ministry. Not only the ministry of Jesus but the "believing ones" that follow him.

### Mark 1:34
34 Then He healed many who were sick with various diseases, and cast out many demons; and He did not allow the demons to speak, because they knew Him.   *NKJV*

### Mark 3:10
10 For He healed many, so that as many as had afflictions pressed about Him to touch Him.  *NKJV*

## Mark 5:21-43

21 Now when Jesus had crossed over again by boat to the other side, a great multitude gathered to Him; and He was by the sea. 22 And behold, one of the rulers of the synagogue came, Jairus by name. And when he saw Him, he fell at His feet 23 and begged Him earnestly, saying, "My little daughter lies at the point of death. Come and lay Your hands on her, that she may be healed, and she will live." 24 So Jesus went with him, and a great multitude followed Him and thronged Him.

25 Now a certain woman had a flow of blood for twelve years, 26 and had suffered many things from many physicians. She had spent all that she had and was no better, but rather grew worse. 27 When she heard about Jesus, she came behind Him in the crowd and touched His garment; 28 for she said, "If only I may touch His clothes, I shall be made well." 29 Immediately the fountain of her blood was dried up, and she felt in her body that she was healed of the affliction. 30 And Jesus, immediately knowing in Himself that power had gone out of Him, turned around in the crowd and said, "Who touched My clothes?" 31 But His disciples said to Him, "You see the multitude thronging You, and You say, 'Who touched Me?' " 32 And He looked around to see her who had done this thing. 33 But the woman, fearing and trembling, knowing what had happened to her, came and fell down before Him and told Him the whole truth. 34 And He said to her, "Daughter, your faith has made you well. Go in peace, and be healed of your affliction."

35 While He was still speaking, some came from the ruler of the synagogue's house who said, "Your daughter is dead. Why

trouble the Teacher any further?" ³⁶ As soon as Jesus heard the word that was spoken, He said to the ruler of the synagogue, "Do not be afraid; only believe." ³⁷ And He permitted no one to follow Him except Peter, James, and John the brother of James. ³⁸ Then He came to the house of the ruler of the synagogue, and saw a tumult and those who wept and wailed loudly. ³⁹ When He came in, He said to them, "Why make this commotion and weep? The child is not dead, but sleeping." ⁴⁰ And they ridiculed Him. But when He had put them all outside, He took the father and the mother of the child, and those who were with Him, and entered where the child was lying. ⁴¹ Then He took the child by the hand, and said to her, "Talitha, cumi," which is translated, "Little girl, I say to you, arise." ⁴² Immediately the girl arose and walked, for she was twelve years of age. And they were overcome with great amazement. ⁴³ But He commanded them strictly that no one should know it, and said that something should be given her to eat. *NKJV*

### *Mark 6:1-6*

¹ Then He went out from there and came to His own country, and His disciples followed Him. ² And when the Sabbath had come, He began to teach in the synagogue. And many hearing Him were astonished, saying, "Where did this Man get these things? And what wisdom is this which is given to Him, that such mighty works are performed by His hands! ³ Is this not the carpenter, the Son of Mary, and brother of James, Joses, Judas, and Simon? And are not His sisters here with us?" And they were offended at Him. ⁴ But Jesus said to them, "A prophet is not without honor except in his own country, among his own relatives, and in his own house." ⁵ Now He could do no mighty work there, except that He laid His hands

on a few sick people and healed them. <sup>6</sup> And He marveled because of their unbelief. Then He went about the villages in a circuit, teaching.   *NKJV*

### Mark 6:7-13

<sup>7</sup> And He called the twelve to Himself, and began to send them out two by two, and gave them power over unclean spirits. <sup>8</sup> He commanded them to take nothing for the journey except a staff--no bag, no bread, no copper in their money belts-- <sup>9</sup> but to wear sandals, and not to put on two tunics. <sup>10</sup> Also He said to them, "In whatever place you enter a house, stay there till you depart from that place. <sup>11</sup> And whoever will not receive you nor hear you, when you depart from there, shake off the dust under your feet as a testimony against them. Assuredly, I say to you, it will be more tolerable for Sodom and Gomorrah in the day of judgment than for that city!" <sup>12</sup> So they went out and preached that people should repent. <sup>13</sup> And they cast out many demons, and anointed with oil many who were sick, and healed them.   *NKJV*

### Mark 16:15-18

<sup>15</sup> And He said to them, "Go into all the world and preach the gospel to every creature. <sup>16</sup> He who believes and is baptized will be saved; but he who does not believe will be condemned. <sup>17</sup> And these signs will follow those who believe: In My name they will cast out demons; they will speak with new tongues; <sup>18</sup> they will take up serpents; and if they drink anything deadly, it will by no means hurt them; they will lay hands on the sick, and they will recover."

# HEALING IN THE BOOK OF LUKE

*Chapter 7*

> *Luke 17:19*
> *And He said to him, "Arise, go your way. Your faith has made you well." NKJV*

Luke was a Jewish physician, and friend of a man we later come to know as the Apostle Paul. As a physician, Luke held a level of prestige among the people and was accepted in the circles of the influential (Priests, Lawmakers, Centurions etc.) and his writing is based on facts and witnessed accounts. Luke took the time to detail the situation in chapter eight where Jesus not only heals the daughter of a Jewish Synagogue leader, but also the woman with the 12-year infirmity. For those of us that face long-term chronic illnesses, Luke's account speaks to the fact that Jesus can heal that which we have carried for a long time.

### Luke 4:40
⁴⁰ When the sun was setting, all those who had any that were sick with various diseases brought them to Him; and He laid His hands on every one of them and healed them. *NKJV*

### Luke 5:15

[15] However, the report went around concerning Him all the more; and great multitudes came together to hear, and to be healed by Him of their infirmities.   *NKJV*

### Luke 6:17-19

[17] And He came down with them and stood on a level place with a crowd of His disciples and a great multitude of people from all Judea and Jerusalem, and from the seacoast of Tyre and Sidon, who came to hear Him and be healed of their diseases, [18] as well as those who were tormented with unclean spirits. And they were healed. [19] And the whole multitude sought to touch Him, for power went out from Him and healed them all.

### Luke 7:2-10

[2] And a certain centurion's servant, who was dear to him, was sick and ready to die. [3] So when he heard about Jesus, he sent elders of the Jews to Him, pleading with Him to come and heal his servant. [4] And when they came to Jesus, they begged Him earnestly, saying that the one for whom He should do this was deserving, [5] for he loves our nation, and has built us a synagogue." [6] Then Jesus went with them. And when He was already not far from the house, the centurion sent friends to Him, saying to Him, "Lord, do not trouble Yourself, for I am not worthy that You should enter under my roof. [7] Therefore I did not even think myself worthy to come to You. But say the word, and my servant will be healed. [8] For I also am a man placed under authority, having soldiers under me. And I say to one, 'Go,' and he goes; and to another, 'Come,' and he

comes; and to my servant, 'Do this,' and he does it." ⁹ When Jesus heard these things, He marveled at him, and turned around and said to the crowd that followed Him, "I say to you, I have not found such great faith, not even in Israel!" ¹⁰ And those who were sent, returning to the house, found the servant well who had been sick.   *NKJV*


### Luke 8:1-3

¹ Now it came to pass, afterward, that He went through every city and village, preaching and bringing the glad tidings of the kingdom of God. And the twelve were with Him, ² and certain women who had been healed of evil spirits and infirmities--Mary called Magdalene, out of whom had come seven demons, ³ and Joanna the wife of Chuza, Herod's steward, and Susanna, and many others who provided for Him from their substance.   *NKJV*


### Luke 8:40-56

⁴⁰ So it was, when Jesus returned, that the multitude welcomed Him, for they were all waiting for Him. ⁴¹ And behold, there came a man named Jairus, and he was a ruler of the synagogue. And he fell down at Jesus' feet and begged Him to come to his house, ⁴² for he had an only daughter about twelve years of age, and she was dying. But as He went, the multitudes thronged Him. ⁴³ Now a woman, having a flow of blood for twelve years, who had spent all her livelihood on physicians and could not be healed by any, ⁴⁴ came from behind and touched the border of His garment. And immediately her flow of blood stopped. ⁴⁵ And Jesus said, "Who touched Me?" When all denied it, Peter and those with

him said, "Master, the multitudes throng and press You, and You say, 'Who touched Me?' " [46] But Jesus said, "Somebody touched Me, for I perceived power going out from Me." [47] Now when the woman saw that she was not hidden, she came trembling; and falling down before Him, she declared to Him in the presence of all the people the reason she had touched Him and how she was healed immediately. [48] And He said to her, "Daughter, be of good cheer; your faith has made you well. Go in peace." [49] While He was still speaking, someone came from the ruler of the synagogue's house, saying to him, "Your daughter is dead. Do not trouble the Teacher." [50] But when Jesus heard it, He answered him, saying, "Do not be afraid; only believe, and she will be made well." [51] When He came into the house, He permitted no one to go in except Peter, James, and John, and the father and mother of the girl. [52] Now all wept and mourned for her; but He said, "Do not weep; she is not dead, but sleeping." [53] And they ridiculed Him, knowing that she was dead. [54] But He put them all outside, took her by the hand and called, saying, "Little girl, arise." [55] Then her spirit returned, and she arose immediately. And He commanded that she be given something to eat. [56] And her parents were astonished, but He charged them to tell no one what had happened. *NKJV*

### Luke 9:11-12
[11] But when the multitudes knew it, they followed Him; and He received them and spoke to them about the kingdom of God, and healed those who had need of healing. *NKJV*

## Luke 9:37-42

[37] Now it happened on the next day, when they had come down from the mountain, that a great multitude met Him. [38] Suddenly a man from the multitude cried out, saying, "Teacher, I implore You, look on my son, for he is my only child. [39] And behold, a spirit seizes him, and he suddenly cries out; it convulses him so that he foams at the mouth, and it departs from him with great difficulty, bruising him. [40] So I implored Your disciples to cast it out, but they could not." [41] Then Jesus answered and said, "O faithless and perverse generation, how long shall I be with you and bear with you? Bring your son here." [42] And as he was still coming, the demon threw him down and convulsed him. Then Jesus rebuked the unclean spirit, healed the child, and gave him back to his father. *NKJV*


## Luke 9:1-6

[1] Then He called His twelve disciples together and gave them power and authority over all demons, and to cure diseases. [2] He sent them to preach the kingdom of God and to heal the sick. [3] And He said to them, "Take nothing for the journey, neither staffs nor bag nor bread nor money; and do not have two tunics apiece. [4] Whatever house you enter, stay there, and from there depart. [5] And whoever will not receive you, when you go out of that city, shake off the very dust from your feet as a testimony against them." [6] So they departed and went through the towns, preaching the gospel and healing everywhere. *NKJV*

### Luke 10:1-9

[1] After these things the Lord appointed seventy others also, and sent them two by two before His face into every city and place where He Himself was about to go. [2] Then He said to them, "The harvest truly is great, but the laborers are few; therefore pray the Lord of the harvest to send out laborers into His harvest. [3] Go your way; behold, I send you out as lambs among wolves. [4] Carry neither money bag, knapsack, nor sandals; and greet no one along the road. [5] But whatever house you enter, first say, 'Peace to this house.' [6] And if a son of peace is there, your peace will rest on it; if not, it will return to you. [7] And remain in the same house, eating and drinking such things as they give, for the laborer is worthy of his wages. Do not go from house to house. [8] Whatever city you enter, and they receive you, eat such things as are set before you. [9] And heal the sick there, and say to them, 'The kingdom of God has come near to you.' *NKJV*

### Luke 13:10-17

[10] Now He was teaching in one of the synagogues on the Sabbath. [11] And behold, there was a woman who had a spirit of infirmity eighteen years, and was bent over and could in no way raise herself up. [12] But when Jesus saw her, He called her to Him and said to her, "Woman, you are loosed from your infirmity." [13] And He laid His hands on her, and immediately she was made straight, and glorified God. [14] But the ruler of the synagogue answered with indignation, because Jesus had healed on the Sabbath; and he said to the crowd, "There are six days on which men ought to work; therefore come and be healed on them, and not on the Sabbath day." [15] The Lord then answered him and said, "Hypocrite! Does not each one of you

on the Sabbath loose his ox or donkey from the stall, and lead it away to water it? ¹⁶ So ought not this woman, being a daughter of Abraham, whom Satan has bound--think of it-- for eighteen years, be loosed from this bond on the Sabbath?" ¹⁷ And when He said these things, all His adversaries were put to shame; and all the multitude rejoiced for all the glorious things that were done by Him.   *NKJV*


## *Luke 14:1-6*

¹ Now it happened, as He went into the house of one of the rulers of the Pharisees to eat bread on the Sabbath, that they watched Him closely. ² And behold, there was a certain man before Him who had dropsy. ³ And Jesus, answering, spoke to the lawyers and Pharisees, saying, "Is it lawful to heal on the Sabbath?" ⁴ But they kept silent. And He took him and healed him, and let him go. ⁵ Then He answered them, saying, "Which of you, having a donkey or an ox that has fallen into a pit, will not immediately pull him out on the Sabbath day?" ⁶ And they could not answer Him regarding these things. *NKJV*


## *Luke 17:11-19*

¹¹ Now it happened as He went to Jerusalem that He passed through the midst of Samaria and Galilee. ¹² Then as He entered a certain village, there met Him ten men who were lepers, who stood afar off. ¹³ And they lifted up their voices and said, "Jesus, Master, have mercy on us!" ¹⁴ So when He saw them, He said to them, "Go, show yourselves to the priests." And so it was that as they went, they were cleansed. ¹⁵ And one of them, when he saw that he was healed, returned,

and with a loud voice glorified God, ¹⁶ and fell down on his face at His feet, giving Him thanks. And he was a Samaritan. ¹⁷ So Jesus answered and said, "Were there not ten cleansed? But where are the nine? ¹⁸ Were there not any found who returned to give glory to God except this foreigner?" ¹⁹ And He said to him, "Arise, go your way. Your faith has made you well." *NKJV*

### Luke 22:50-51
⁵⁰ And one of them struck the servant of the high priest and cut off his right ear. ⁵¹ But Jesus answered and said, "Permit even this." And He touched his ear and healed him. *NKJV*

# HEALING IN THE BOOK OF JOHN

*Chapter 8*

> *John 5:8-9*
> *Jesus said to him, "Rise, take up your bed and walk." ⁹ And immediately the man was made well, took up his bed, and walked. And that day was the Sabbath.*

John referred to himself as the disciple whom Jesus loved. He and his brother James were part of Jesus' "inner circle" along with Peter. As a disciple that walked closely with Jesus, John witnessed three significant healings as a sign of the reality of Him coming as the Messiah who brings redemption and healing to the world.

### John 4:46-54

⁴⁶ So Jesus came again to Cana of Galilee where He had made the water wine. And there was a certain nobleman whose son was sick at Capernaum. ⁴⁷ When he heard that Jesus had come out of Judea into Galilee, he went to Him and implored Him to come down and heal his son, for he was at the point of death. ⁴⁸ Then Jesus said to him, "Unless you people see signs and wonders, you will by no means believe." ⁴⁹ The nobleman said to Him, "Sir, come down before my child dies!" ⁵⁰ Jesus

said to him, "Go your way; your son lives." So the man believed the word that Jesus spoke to him, and he went his way. [51] And as he was now going down, his servants met him and told him, saying, "Your son lives!" [52] Then he inquired of them the hour when he got better. And they said to him, "Yesterday at the seventh hour the fever left him." [53] So the father knew that it was at the same hour in which Jesus said to him, "Your son lives." And he himself believed, and his whole household. [54] This again is the second sign Jesus did when He had come out of Judea into Galilee. *NKJV*

### *John 5:1-15*

[1] After this there was a feast of the Jews, and Jesus went up to Jerusalem. [2] Now there is in Jerusalem by the Sheep Gate a pool, which is called in Hebrew, Bethesda, having five porches. [3] In these lay a great multitude of sick people, blind, lame, paralyzed, waiting for the moving of the water. [4] For an angel went down at a certain time into the pool and stirred up the water; then whoever stepped in first, after the stirring of the water, was made well of whatever disease he had. [5] Now a certain man was there who had an infirmity thirty-eight years. [6] When Jesus saw him lying there, and knew that he already had been in that condition a long time, He said to him, "Do you want to be made well?" [7] The sick man answered Him, "Sir, I have no man to put me into the pool when the water is stirred up; but while I am coming, another steps down before me." [8] Jesus said to him, "Rise, take up your bed and walk." [9] And immediately the man was made well, took up his bed, and walked. And that day was the Sabbath.

<sup>10</sup> The Jews therefore said to him who was cured, "It is the Sabbath; it is not lawful for you to carry your bed." <sup>11</sup> He answered them, "He who made me well said to me, 'Take up your bed and walk.' " <sup>12</sup> Then they asked him, "Who is the Man who said to you, 'Take up your bed and walk'?" <sup>13</sup> But the one who was healed did not know who it was, for Jesus had withdrawn, a multitude being in that place. <sup>14</sup> Afterward Jesus found him in the temple, and said to him, "See, you have been made well. Sin no more, lest a worse thing come upon you." <sup>15</sup> The man departed and told the Jews that it was Jesus who had made him well.    *NKJV*

### *John 9:1-7*

<sup>1</sup> Now as Jesus passed by, He saw a man who was blind from birth. <sup>2</sup> And His disciples asked Him, saying, "Rabbi, who sinned, this man or his parents, that he was born blind?" <sup>3</sup> Jesus answered, "Neither this man nor his parents sinned, but that the works of God should be revealed in him. <sup>4</sup> I must work the works of Him who sent Me while it is day; the night is coming when no one can work. <sup>5</sup> As long as I am in the world, I am the light of the world." <sup>6</sup> When He had said these things, He spat on the ground and made clay with the saliva; and He anointed the eyes of the blind man with the clay. <sup>7</sup> And He said to him, "Go, wash in the pool of Siloam" (which is translated, Sent). So he went and washed, and came back seeing.    *NKJV*

# HEALING IN THE BOOK OF ACTS

*Chapter 9*

> Acts 10:38
> *"how God anointed Jesus of Nazareth with the Holy Spirit and power, who went about doing good and healing all who were oppressed of the devil, for God was with Him. NKJV*

The Book of Acts was written by Luke the physician and records the actions taken by the Apostles after the resurrection of Jesus. It is important to understand that not only the actions of the original 11 disciples are recorded, but also the work and actions of the second generation of apostles that were not disciples directly trained by Jesus. These include Silas, Barnabus, and Saul of Tarsus who would become the Apostle Paul.

This is important to note because this truth means that God will manifest Himself as a healer through us the same way that He manifested Himself as a healer through the original apostles.

### *Acts 3:1-10*

¹ Now Peter and John went up together to the temple at the hour of prayer, the ninth hour. ² And a certain man lame from his mother's womb was carried, whom they laid daily at the gate of the temple which is called Beautiful, to ask alms from those who entered the temple; ³ who, seeing Peter and John about to go into the temple, asked for alms. ⁴ And fixing his eyes on him, with John, Peter said, "Look at us." ⁵ So he gave them his attention, expecting to receive something from them. ⁶ Then Peter said, "Silver and gold I do not have, but what I do have I give you: In the name of Jesus Christ of Nazareth, rise up and walk." ⁷ And he took him by the right hand and lifted him up, and immediately his feet and ankle bones received strength. ⁸ So he, leaping up, stood and walked and entered the temple with them--walking, leaping, and praising God. ⁹ And all the people saw him walking and praising God. ¹⁰ Then they knew that it was he who sat begging alms at the Beautiful Gate of the temple; and they were filled with wonder and amazement at what had happened to him.   *NKJV*

### Acts 4:29-31

²⁹ Now, Lord, look on their threats, and grant to Your servants that with all boldness they may speak Your word, ³⁰ by stretching out Your hand to heal, and that signs and wonders may be done through the name of Your holy Servant Jesus." ³¹ And when they had prayed, the place where they were assembled together was shaken; and they were all filled with the Holy Spirit, and they spoke the word of God with boldness. *NKJV*

### Acts 5:14-16

[14] And believers were increasingly added to the Lord, multitudes of both men and women, [15] so that they brought the sick out into the streets and laid them on beds and couches, that at least the shadow of Peter passing by might fall on some of them. [16] Also a multitude gathered from the surrounding cities to Jerusalem, bringing sick people and those who were tormented by unclean spirits, and they were all healed.  *NKJV*

### Acts 8:4-8

[4] Therefore those who were scattered went everywhere preaching the word. [5] Then Philip went down to the city of Samaria and preached Christ to them. [6] And the multitudes with one accord heeded the things spoken by Philip, hearing and seeing the miracles which he did. [7] For unclean spirits, crying with a loud voice, came out of many who were possessed; and many who were paralyzed and lame were healed. [8] And there was great joy in that city.   *NKJV*

### Acts 10:38

"how God anointed Jesus of Nazareth with the Holy Spirit and power, who went about doing good and healing all who were oppressed of he devil, for God was with Him.  *NKJV*

### Acts 14:8-11

[8] And in Lystra a certain man without strength in his feet was sitting, a cripple from his mother's womb, who had never walked. [9] This man heard Paul speaking. Paul, observing him

intently and seeing that he had faith to be healed, [10] said with a loud voice, "Stand up straight on your feet!" And he leaped and walked.   *NKJV*


### Acts 20:7-12

[7] Now on the first day of the week, when the disciples came together to break bread, Paul, ready to depart the next day, spoke to them and continued his message until midnight. [8] There were many lamps in the upper room where they were gathered together. [9] And in a window sat a certain young man named Eutychus, who was sinking into a deep sleep. He was overcome by sleep; and as Paul continued speaking, <u>he fell down from the third story and was taken up dead</u>. [10] But Paul went down, fell on him, and embracing him said, "Do not trouble yourselves, for his life is in him." [11] Now when he (Paul) had come up, had broken bread and eaten, and talked a long while, even till daybreak, he departed. [12] <u>And they brought the young man in alive,</u> and they were not a little comforted.   *NKJV*


### Acts 28:7-9

[7] In that region there was an estate of the leading citizen of the island, whose name was Publius, who received us and entertained us courteously for three days. [8] And it happened that the father of Publius lay sick of a fever and dysentery. Paul went in to him and prayed, and he laid his hands on him and healed him. [9] So when this was done, the rest of those on the island who had diseases also came and were healed.   *NKJV*

***Acts 28:25-27***

²⁵ So when they did not agree among themselves, they departed after Paul had said one word: "The Holy Spirit spoke rightly through Isaiah the prophet to our fathers, ²⁶ saying,

'Go to this people and say:
"Hearing you will hear, and shall not understand;
And seeing you will see, and not perceive;
²⁷ For the hearts of this people have grown dull.
Their ears are hard of hearing,
And their eyes they have closed,
Lest they should see with their eyes and hear with their ears,
Lest they should understand with their hearts and turn,
So that I should heal them." '   *NKJV*

# CONCLUSION

*Chapter 10*

> *Exodus 15:26*
> *For I Am the LORD that healeth thee. KJV*

The conclusion is simple, God wants you well and has empowered us to receive healing as a part of our new covenant with Him. The reality is that at some point this body will face death. But in the meantime, it is God's will that you maintain a well body, strong enough to complete the work that He has ordained you to fulfill.

Your healing testimony not only is a blessing to you, but it is a witness of the power of God that can bring deliverance to others that are coming to God and will lead them to saving grace as their faith in Him is ignited by your story. As God heals you, go and tell of the things that God has done for you. In Luke 8, a man that had been healed by Jesus wanted to begin following as one of His disciples, but Jesus gave the man other instructions.

> *Luke 8:39*
> **"No, go back to your family, and tell them everything God has done for you."** So he went all through the town proclaiming the great things Jesus had done for him. *New Living Translation.*

61

This book is full of information about what the Bible says about Jesus and healing. Now it is time to receive the revelation of healing, activate it in your life by faith, and receive the manifestation of God's healing. Once you receive, begin testifying of who Jesus has now become in your life.

I can't wait to hear your testimony.

# JOURNAL

*Applying the Revelation of Meditation*
*for Healing*

# HEALING CONFESSIONS

*Hebrews 10:23*
*Let us hold fast the profession of our faith without wavering; (for He is faithful that promised;) NKJV*

You have just read a book that has illustrated the healing ministry of Jesus and God's will for you to be well to fulfill your purpose.

As you are reading and meditating on this reality of healing as God's revealed will and the cornerstone of the ministry of Jesus, it is time to activate this reality. Just like a doctor would prescribe (Rx) medication which might have instructions to take daily, let's add the Word as a daily medication to build a spiritual resistance to sickness and disease.

Begin your morning prayer with a personal Rx, declaring what is written and what we believe. Thank the Father for what the Word says. The scriptures you have read and those below are a great foundation to build your faith and guide your personal confession of hope. In the section following the scriptures, is a 21 day journal, with a daily scripture or idea of God's healing power for you.

### James 5:15
[15] And the prayer of faith shall save the sick, and the Lord shall raise him up; and if he have committed sins, they shall be forgiven him.

65

### Romans 8:11

[11] But if the Spirit of him that raised up Jesus from the dead dwell in you, he that raised up Christ from the dead shall also quicken your mortal bodies by his Spirit that dwelleth in you.

### Romans 8:2

[2] For the law of the Spirit of life in Christ Jesus hath made me free from the law of sin and death.

### John 8:36

[36] If the Son therefore shall make you free, ye shall be free indeed.

### 1 John 4:4

[4] Ye are of God, little children, and have overcome them: because greater is he that is in you, than he that is in the world.

### 1 John 3:8

[8] He that committeth sin is of the devil; for the devil sinneth from the beginning. For this purpose the Son of God was manifested, that he might destroy the works of the devil.

### John 14:13-14

[13] And whatsoever ye shall ask in my name, that will I do, that the Father may be glorified in the Son.
[14] If ye shall ask any thing in my name, I will do it.

### Colossians 1:20

[20] And, having made peace through the blood of his cross, by him to reconcile all things unto himself; by him, I say, whether they be things in earth, or things in heaven.

### 2 Corinthians 5:17

[17] Therefore if any man be in Christ, he is a new creature: old things are passed away; behold, all things are become new.

### 1 Corinthians 6:17

[17] But he that is joined unto the Lord is one spirit.

### 1 Corinthians 3:16

[16] Know ye not that ye are the temple of God, and that the Spirit of God dwelleth in you?

### Psalms 107:20

[20] He sent his word, and healed them, and delivered them from their destructions.

### Exodus 15:26

[26] And said, If thou wilt diligently hearken to the voice of the LORD thy God, and wilt do that which is right in his sight, and wilt give ear to his commandments, and keep all his statutes, I will put none of these diseases upon thee, which I have brought upon the Egyptians: for I am the LORD that healeth thee.

### 1 Peter 2:24

[24] Who his own self bare our sins in his own body on the tree, that we, being dead to sins, should live unto righteousness: by whose stripes ye were healed.

### 2 Corinthians 2:14

14 Now thanks be to God who always leads us in triumph in Christ, and through us diffuses the fragrance of His knowledge in every place. *NKJV*

### Romans 8:37

37 Nay, in all these things we are more than conquerors through him that loved us.

### 2 Corinthians 10:5

5 Casting down imaginations, and every high thing that exalteth itself against the knowledge of God, and bringing into captivity every thought to the obedience of Christ;

# 21 DAY MEDITATIONS FOR HEALING

> *James 2:20*
> *But do you want to know, O foolish man, that faith without works is dead? NKJV*

As God reveals Himself as Jehovah Rapha (Healer **Exodus 15:26**) we must grow in our Wisdom concerning maintaining health: spiritual, physical, mental, and emotional. The foundation begins with three concepts to renew our minds:

- I must accept *the revelation that "Healing is the Will of God"*
- I must create *an atmosphere/environment for healing*
  - **Faith/Believe** – Believe that Healing is the Will of God according to the Word
  - **Meditation** – Maintain a favorable Meditation on the Word. **Joshua 1:8-9**
  - **Rest** in the Truth of the Word. **Hebrews 4:9-14**
  - **Forgive** through the Love of God. **Romans 5:5**
  - **Intercede** for those in trouble. **James 5:14-20**
- I must receive and embrace *God's provision for overcoming the fear of death* – **Hebrews 2:14-18**

Using the instructions for scriptural meditation found in Chapter 3, activate your meditation by using the daily journal below. As you prepare to meditate on the Word of God please remember the following:

- Read the daily scripture and meditate on what you read by documenting your thoughts to the four daily questions. Take your time and really meditate about what you are reading. Although we live a life of faith, the scriptures lead us to a logical conclusion concerning God's will towards healing.

- Pray for God to enlighten your mind to the truth concerning His will in the area of Healing. If it is true, then let God persuade you through His Word. What people say apart from the scriptures is only conceptual and personal opinion. Trust in God and His Word.

- Act on God's instructions immediately. As God communicates back to you be prepared to respond immediately.

- As Joshua 1:8 says, do not let the word depart from your mouth. Speak God's Word concerning healing. Boldly declare it to your body. Declare it to your mind. Confess the Word to God, as it says in Hebrews 4:14 "...let us hold fast our confession".

- As you confess the Word, say out loud what the Word is saying to you. Faith comes by hearing, and as you hear yourself your faith will increase.

- According to II Corinthians 10:4-5, reject any thoughts or confessions that go against what God reveals to you from His Word.

The daily meditations in the next several pages will start you on the path of moving toward health.

Day 1.    Healing is God's Character - **Exodus 15:26, Numbers 23:19** – God is not a man that He should lie.

Day 2.    Healing was part of Jesus' earthly ministry – **Luke 4:18-19**

Day 3.    The Word is God's medicine. **Proverbs 4:20-22, Psalm 107:19-21**

Day 4.    Healing is included in the new birth and is connected to fulfilling our purpose. **Matthew 8:16-17, Galatians 3:13**

Day 5.    Healing is for the whole person (triune – Spirit, Soul, and Body) 1 **Thessalonians 5:23**

Day 6.    Healing is a benefit of serving God. **Psalm 102:1-5**

Day 7.    Worship is a therapy for healing (Strong's word NT:2323 – Therapeuo – to heal)

Day 8.    Faith is an incubator for healing. Sozo – **Matthew 9:22, Mark 10:52**

Day 9.     Jesus, because of His love for us, gives us sozo
           through grace.  **Ephesians 2:4-8**

Day 10.    Jesus, because of His love for us brought us (aid-
           help) to us to free us from the fear of death.
           **Hebrews 2:14-16**

Day 11.    Forgiveness and healing are connected.  **Luke 5:20-
           25**

Day 12.    You have been empowered to love and forgive
           through the Holy Spirit who was given to us.
           **Romans 5:5, John 20:21-23**

Day 13.    You have been given the power to choose your
           meditation.  **Philippians 4:8**

Day 14.    Success in any endeavor (including healing) is
           impacted by our meditation.  **Joshua 1:8-9**

Day 15.    Meditation renews the mind, and releases the perfect
           will of God in our lives.  **Romans 12:2-3**

Day 16.    Rest is a promise to us who believe.  **Hebrews 4:9-14**

Day 17.    Rest lowers the levels of stress and anxiety in our
           lives.  **Philippians 4:6-8**

Day 18.    Praying for one another brings healing. **James 5:16**

Day 19.    Praying for those that do not understand you, brings healing and restoration. **Job 42:10**

Day 20.    Fasting and praying for others causes and open door for our healing. **Isaiah 58:6-8**

Day 21.    God has a purpose for your life. **Jeremiah 29:11**

# Day 1

Read the daily thought and scripture, meditate and pray over them, then document your thoughts in the space below. Now that you have this truth, how will you respond? If necessary, use a separate sheet of paper or a journal to fully express your answers.

> *Healing is God's Character **Exodus 15:26, Numbers 23:19*** *– God is not a man that He should lie.*

What did you hear?

What do you think?

What will you do?

# Day 2

Read the daily thought and scripture, meditate and pray over them, then document your thoughts in the space below. Now that you have this truth, how will you respond? If necessary, use a separate sheet of paper or a journal to fully express your answers.

> *Healing was part of Jesus' earthly ministry –* ***Luke 4:18-19***

What did you hear?

What do you think?

What will you do?

# Day 3

Read the daily thought and scripture, meditate and pray over them, then document your thoughts in the space below. Now that you have this truth, how will you respond? If necessary, use a separate sheet of paper or a journal to fully express your answers.

> *The Word is God's medicine.* Proverbs 4:20-22, Psalm 107:19-21

What did you hear?

What do you think?

What will you do?

# Day 4

Read the daily thought and scripture, meditate and pray over them, then document your thoughts in the space below. Now that you have this truth, how will you respond? If necessary, use a separate sheet of paper or a journal to fully express your answers.

> *Healing is included in the new birth and is connected to fulfilling our purpose.* ***Matthew 8:16-17, Galatians 3:13***

What did you hear?

What do you think?

What will you do?

# Day 5

Read the daily thought and scripture, meditate and pray over them, then document your thoughts in the space below. Now that you have this truth, how will you respond? If necessary, use a separate sheet of paper or a journal to fully express your answers.

> *Healing is for the whole person (triune − Spirit, Soul, and Body)* 1 ***Thessalonians 5:23***

What did you hear?




What do you think?




What will you do?

# Day 6

Read the daily thought and scripture, meditate and pray over them, then document your thoughts in the space below. Now that you have this truth, how will you respond? If necessary, use a separate sheet of paper or a journal to fully express your answers.

| *Healing is a benefit of serving God.* ***Psalm 102:1-5***

---

What did you hear?




What do you think?




What will you do?

---

# Day 7

Read the daily thought, meditate and pray over it, then document your thoughts in the space below. Now that you have this truth, how will you respond? If necessary, use a separate sheet of paper or a journal to fully express your answers.

> *Worship is a therapy for healing (Strong's word NT:2323 – Therapeuo – to heal)*

What did you hear?




What do you think?




What will you do?

# Day 8

Read the daily thought and scripture, meditate and pray over them, then document your thoughts in the space below. Now that you have this truth, how will you respond? If necessary, use a separate sheet of paper or a journal to fully express your answers.

> *Faith is an incubator for healing. Sozo –* ***Matthew 9:22,*** ***Mark 10:52***

What did you hear?




What do you think?




What will you do?

# Day 9

Read the daily thought and scripture, meditate and pray over them, then document your thoughts in the space below. Now that you have this truth, how will you respond? If necessary, use a separate sheet of paper or a journal to fully express your answers.

> *Jesus, because of His love for us, gives us sozo through grace.*
> **Ephesians 2:4-8**

What did you hear?

What do you think?

What will you do?

# Day 10

Read the daily thought and scripture, meditate and pray over them, then document your thoughts in the space below. Now that you have this truth, how will you respond? If necessary, use a separate sheet of paper or a journal to fully express your answers.

> *Jesus, because of His love for us brought us (aid-help) to us to free us from the fear of death.* ***Hebrews 2:14-16***

What did you hear?

What do you think?

What will you do?

# Day 11

Read the daily thought and scripture, meditate and pray over them, then document your thoughts in the space below. Now that you have this truth, how will you respond? If necessary, use a separate sheet of paper or a journal to fully express your answers.

| *Forgiveness and healing are connected.* ***Luke 5:20-25***

What did you hear?

What do you think?

What will you do?

# Day 12

Read the daily thought and scripture, meditate and pray over them, then document your thoughts in the space below. Now that you have this truth, how will you respond? If necessary, use a separate sheet of paper or a journal to fully express your answers.

> *You have been empowered to love and forgive through the Holy Spirit who was given to us.* ***Romans 5:5, John 20:21-23***

What did you hear?

What do you think?

What will you do?

# Day 13

Read the daily thought and scripture, meditate and pray over them, then document your thoughts in the space below. Now that you have this truth, how will you respond? If necessary, use a separate sheet of paper or a journal to fully express your answers.

> *You have been given the power to choose your meditation.*
> ***Philippians 4:8***

What did you hear?

What do you think?

What will you do?

# Day 14

Read the daily thought and scripture, meditate and pray over them, then document your thoughts in the space below. Now that you have this truth, how will you respond? If necessary, use a separate sheet of paper or a journal to fully express your answers.

> *Success in any endeavor (including healing) is impacted by our meditation.* **Joshua 1:8-9**

What did you hear?

What do you think?

What will you do?

# Day 15

Read the daily thought and scripture, meditate and pray over them, then document your thoughts in the space below. Now that you have this truth, how will you respond? If necessary, use a separate sheet of paper or a journal to fully express your answers.

> *Meditation renews the mind, and releases the perfect will of God in our lives.* ***Romans 12:2-3***

What did you hear?

What do you think?

What will you do?

# Day 16

Read the daily thought and scripture, meditate and pray over them, then document your thoughts in the space below. Now that you have this truth, how will you respond? If necessary, use a separate sheet of paper or a journal to fully express your answers.

> Rest is a promise to us who believe. **Hebrews 4:9-14**

What did you hear?

What do you think?

What will you do?

# Day 17

Read the daily thought and scripture, meditate and pray over them, then document your thoughts in the space below. Now that you have this truth, how will you respond? If necessary, use a separate sheet of paper or a journal to fully express your answers.

*Rest lowers the levels of stress and anxiety in our lives.*
***Philippians 4:6-8***

What did you hear?

What do you think?

What will you do?

# Day 18

Read the daily thought and scripture, meditate and pray over them, then document your thoughts in the space below. Now that you have this truth, how will you respond? If necessary, use a separate sheet of paper or a journal to fully express your answers.

*Praying for one another brings healing. **James 5:16***

---

What did you hear?


What do you think?


What will you do?

---

# Day 19

Read the daily thought and scripture, meditate and pray over them, then document your thoughts in the space below. Now that you have this truth, how will you respond? If necessary, use a separate sheet of paper or a journal to fully express your answers.

> *Praying for those that do not understand you, brings healing and restoration.* ***Job 42:10***

What did you hear?

What do you think?

What will you do?

# Day 20

Read the daily thought and scripture, meditate and pray over them, then document your thoughts in the space below. Now that you have this truth, how will you respond? If necessary, use a separate sheet of paper or a journal to fully express your answers.

> *Fasting and praying for others causes an open door for our healing.* ***Isaiah 58:6-8***

What did you hear?

What do you think?

What will you do?

# Day 21

Read the daily thought and scripture, meditate and pray over them, then document your thoughts in the space below. Now that you have this truth, how will you respond? If necessary, use a separate sheet of paper or a journal to fully express your answers.

| *God has a purpose for your life.* ***Jeremiah 29:11***

What did you hear?

What do you think?

What will you do?

# ABOUT THE AUTHOR

Derry L. Moten, is a multi-gifted adult educator and leader in business and Christian ministry. For more than thirty years he has successfully served thousands of people through his efforts in ministry, Human Resources, and Workforce Development for youth and adults.

God has revealed tremendous insight through Derry on how to release "Divine Wisdom to solve real world problems." Over the years he has successfully taught these Life of Faith principles to people searching for practical ways to experience balanced and purpose filled lives. These teachings are the foundation of Abundant Life Worship Center, in Vallejo, California, where he and his "Proverbs 31" wife Tammie serve as Lead Pastors.

Derry and Tammie have been married for over 30 years and with pride have raised three successful young adults; Derry Alexander, Micalia, and Maya.

# CONNECT WITH US

Connect with Pastor Derry and Tammie at Abundant Life Worship Center through our website and Social Media.

Abundant Life Worship Center
P.O. Box 6059
Vallejo, California 94591
(707) 644-8956

Visit **www.abundantlifeworship.net**

**Facebook.com/abundantlifeworship.net**
**Twitter.com/alwcnorthbay**

Share your testimony with us
**http://abundantlifeworship.net/alwc-prayer-network/**

Abundant Life Worship Center

# MEDITATIONS FOR HEALING

*Activating the Power of Scriptural Meditation for Divine Healing*

## Derry L. Moten

www.ingramcontent.com/pod-product-compliance
Lightning Source LLC
Chambersburg PA
CBHW071454070426
42452CB00039B/1356